ANGEL WITH A
LOUD VOICE

BURNT OFFERING

DEDICATION

This book is dedicated with my sincere gratitude to my daughter and son and real or online sisters and brothers whose support of my story help make this book possible.

Sincerely,
Burnt Offering

AUTHOR'S BIO

Pen Named Burnt-Offering (Heb. 10:7-10)

Burnt Offering was born in New Rochelle, NY, as the third of five daughters from parents with both Negro and Native American Indian ancestry. From infancy, she never slept at night and as she got older became more of a loner, or a Wednesday's child of Woe with a typical middle child syndrome. However, she always enjoyed solving paradoxical puzzles or poems and revealing hidden meanings to riddles by showing a different viewpoint to songs.

When Burnt was 10 years old, she told her mother she would marry her cousin's next-door neighbor, who lived in her mother's hometown in Delaware. Although she was espoused to her high school lover, Burnt eloped instead with her cousin's neighbor and married him on April Fools' Day. His sister and she shared the same age and birthday. He was a radioman on a submarine and lived in New London, Connecticut. After relocation to Monterey, California, they returned to Connecticut. Upon leaving the Navy, they moved to Rockville, Maryland, and separated shortly after as they had no children. While vacationing out of the country with two of her sisters, Burnt was told he had died unexpectedly at Holy Cross Hospital. Six years later, Burnt married James, a brother in Christ, and gave birth to two children, a daughter and a son.

Prior to the first black Million Man March in 1995, Burnt received her Indigenous vision. Her belief in God and life took a drastic change ever since. She recalls her mother calling her to relay that Minister Farrakhan was repeating what she had said to her weeks earlier. Burnt divorced her husband in 2004, shortly before he had a massive stroke on his birthday, and he died in 2017. Burnt has dedicated the past 40 years to studying her heritage and the King James Version of the Holy Bible.

Contents

DEDICATION i

AUTHOR'S BIO..ii

PREFACE 1

SATAN'S SWORN TESTIMONY 3

MY GENESIS..9

THE ALPHA BETA CHART DIE-A-LOGUE 17

THE ALPHA-BETA CHART..18

THE ALPHA-BETA CHART..20

DIVINE TRINITY MOTHER FAMILY............................22

MYSTERY THE MOTHER OF HARLOTS AND ABOMINATION
OF THE EARTH 29

GREAT MYSTERY REVEALED 32

YOUR MAMA IS SO FAT 38

GOD'S DIRTY WORK...42

WOMEN SAVED OR RISEN FROM DEAD....................44

VOICES OF OTHER ANGELS 47

SATAN'S DAY IN COURT..49

PRESENTED QUESTIONS 51

AND LIVED HAPPILY, FOREVER AFTER.....................54

THE WEDDING TO END ALL TIME..............................56

PREFACE

Satan's Review on the King James Version (KJV) of the Holy Bible

As told by the Black Sheep in the Trinity Family

This is a true story and testimony of a black Christian woman who says she is Satan risen, reborn and transformed into flesh as the Daughter of God, Twin Sister and Bride of Jesus Christ.

(Rev.1:2, 3:9, 5:1-5, 10:7-10, 14:6-7, 19:7-10, 21:9, 22:16)

Satan uses bible scripture "male and female made he them" along with Charles Mendel's Human Gender theory (Xy=males and XX= females) to prove we all come from the dark heavenly, water, and womb of a Goddess=X(y+X)X. Due to the prominence of twin sons born in the bible, this X(y+X)X theory instead shows a Mother with twin boy and girl within Her womb as the real Trinity. Although the word Trinity is not in the bible, the X(y+X)X theory shows Jesus Christ as the only (y) or son of God or male, and the center X as a female, as God's daughter, Satan, aka the Anti-Christ.

Jesus used many metonyms and parables in the bible. For example, the Trinity, aka the Father, Son, and Holy Ghost, is One. Then the Mother, Daughter, and Holy Ghostess is the other One that "bear witness in earth." When Jesus said "I and my father are one," he meant the X and y are one human, and the mother and daughter XX are another. Not that he and the father were the same person. Individually, the Father=X, Son=(y), and Mother=X and Daughter=X would be a qua-trinity, not a trinity. But as you can see, all the Xs are female, including the father. So, my X(y+X)X theory of the real Trinity is a biblical, literal, mathematical and scientific parallel analogy.

Math. 28:19 "Go ye therefore and teach all nations baptizing them in the name of the Father and of the Son and of the Holy Ghost."

1

1 John 5:7 "For there are three that bear record in heaven the father the word and the holy ghost and these three are one. And there are three that bear witness in earth the spirit, the water, and the blood and these three are one."

SATAN'S SWORN TESTIMONY

This is the testimony of Satan now risen and reborn into the flesh of a black Christian woman. As Satan, I am the daughter of God, twin sister, and the espoused bride of Jesus Christ. I am the 1 in 100 lost black sheep in the Trinity family, aka God's other kid. I am the treacherous backsliding sister of Jesus who also played the part of the harlot. Although I play many roles, it's more like Jesus Christ is the President and I am the Vice President and his Secret Tarry. I took his dictation and wrote down what he said, like in the book "The Spook Who Sat Next to the Door." God devised this master plan ever since Gen.1:26-27 when God said, "Let us make man in our own image, after our likeness and let them have dominion… male and female made he them." God planned for the only son and daughter to live happily forever after the fall of All Damn Arrogant Men (ADAM). God Kept It Simple Sons (KISS)ed us by using the human body of a woman to let us know where we really came from. To be clear, I call God Almighty, She or Her, Jesus Christ He or Him, and I, like God, am a She or Her. I use KJV bible scriptures throughout the book to prove my points. Please do not use the New Improved Versions, aka NIVs, due to the word changes and so we can stay on the same page. Plus, no man on earth can improve on a thing he never really understood in the 1st place.

> Hab. 1:5 "Behold ye among the heathen, and regard, and wonder marvelously: for I will work a work in your days, which ye will not believe, though it be told you.

> Hab. 2:1-3 "I will stand upon my watch, and set me upon the tower, and will watch to see what he will say unto me, and what I shall answer when I am reproved. And the Lord answered me, and said, Write the vision, and make it plain upon tables, that he may run that readeth it. For the vision is yet for an appointed time, but at the end it shall speak, and not lie though it tarry, wait for it; because it will surely come, it will not tarry."

Jer. 8:7 "Yea, The stork in heaven knoweth her appointed time..."

So, with my Hand on the Bible, I promise to tell the whole truth and nothing but the truth, so help me God this time. As God is my only witness, I have been working for God all along. Since we are in the last days or times, I can finally come out of my prayer closet. I did not do any of the things Christians blamed on me. The only thing I can guarantee you for sure is that not even A-Bad-Don Pope in Rev.9:11 or the Holy See ever saw me coming.

> Joel 2:16 "Gather the people, sanctify the congregation, assemble the elders, gather the children, and those that suck the breasts: let the bridegroom go forth of his chamber, and the bride out of her closet."

> Rev. 21:9 "And there came unto me one of the seven angels which had the seven vials full of the seven last plagues, and talked with me, saying, Come hither, I will shew thee the bride, the Lamb's wife."

My primary mission is to preach, teach, and share this Good News of Jesus Christ from the North, East, West, and South, and spells NEWS. Jesus' mission was to save the world, but mine was to deceive it. So now, as never before, you can compare His story, traditionally told, to Her story written above and below. Then just go for what you know!

> John 12:28 "Father, glorify thy name. Then came there a voice from heaven, saying, I have both glorified it, and will glorify it again. The people therefore, that stood by, and heard it, said that it thundered: others said, An angel spake to him. Jesus answered and said, <u>this voice came not because of me, but for your sakes.</u>"

> Rev.17:6 "And I saw the woman drunken with the blood of the saints, and with the blood of the martyrs of Jesus: and when I saw her, I wondered with great admiration. <u>And the angel said</u>

unto me, wherefore didst thou marvel? I will tell thee the mystery of the woman, and of the beast that carrieth her, which hath the seven heads and ten horns. The beast that thou sawest was, and is not; and shall ascend out of the bottomless pit, and go into perdition: and they that dwell on the earth shall wonder, whose names were not written in the book of life from the foundation of the world, when they behold the beast that was, and is not, and yet is."

Secondly, the Bad NEWS is I must Warn You To Fear God Almighty, aka the Great and Terrible Day of the Coming of the Lord. So "Ain't Nothing Going On But The Rent" or the bible calls the Final Judgement.

2 Cor. 11:14 "And no marvel; for Satan himself is transformed into an angel of light. Therefore, it is no great thing if his ministers also be..."

Math. 16:4 "A wicked and adulterous generation seeketh after a sign; and there shall no sign be given unto it, but the sign of the prophet Jonas."

Rev. 14:7 "Saying with a loud voice, Fear God, and give glory to him; for the hour of his judgment is come: and worship him that made heaven, and earth, and the sea, and the fountains of waters."

God said in Rom. 12:19 "Vengeance is m(in)e I will repay" but I can clearly see vengeance in **me** or m(in)e as the same thing. Jesus said he was the Alpha and Omega, but I am the second in the midst of the O(**me**)ga. Jesus came not to judge but to save the world and said one would come to judge you. I want to assure everyone that I ab-soul-loot-lye love my God and Job 2. Just keep in mind that before destruction God always sent a warning to people like Noah or Jonah. This book is no different.

John 12:47 "And if any man hear my words, and believe not, I judge him not: <u>for I came not to judge the world, but to save the world</u>. He that rejecteth me, and receiveth not my words, hath one that judgeth him. The <u>word that I have spoken, the same shall judge him in the last day</u>."

Rev. 12:12 "Therefore rejoice, ye heavens, and ye that dwell in them. Woe to the inhabiters of the earth and of the sea! for the devil is come down unto you, having great wrath, because he knoweth that he hath but a short time."

Third, to rudely wake you up and remind you of things you forgot. Although I was the liar and a defeated foe, I have been sent back as the Spirit of Truth. So, I am not the Holy Ghost, but I am a Holy Ghostess, Holy Hostess and/or a Goddess. As the lioness I've been sent to devour and destroy ADAM's fragile male egos. I will also reveal secrets hidden since the beginning of time. This truth may hurt. But if I were you, I would pay close attention to what an "Angel With A Loud Voice" and Her sword drawn has to say to you all.

Luke 21:35 "For as a snare shall it come on all them that dwell on the face of the whole earth."

John 14:26 "But the Comforter, which is the Holy Ghost, whom the Father will send in my name, he shall teach you all things, and bring all things to your remembrance, whatsoever I have said unto you."

Math.12:32 "But whosoever speak against the Holy Ghost it shall not be forgiven him in this world neither in the world to come."

Isn't Mrs. Jesus Christ the same thing as coming in his name? As foretold, there are many false prophets nowadays claiming to be Jesus. But the only sin in the Bible that will not be forgiven is written above.

Even if you believe in reincarnation, you will still be SOL, aka Shit Out of Luck. I know you saw the word he above, but due to men not showing the word *he* when referring to God as s/he or he/r both are implied.

Fourth, I am just A Plain American Indigenous Negro and Native Democratic Assimilated Sister Christian Citizen or A PAIN ND ASCC for short. As a daughter of forefathers: Abraham, Lincoln, and Red Cloud, I know the Bible says "the woman was given both wings of an eagle" to fly into a place prepared by God. This means I was begot or born with a First Amen-demented legal right to proceed and now take flight. Jesus said only the Father in heaven knows the day or hour. But only a Mother knows when it's time to give Birth, Prays Until Something Happens (PUSH), and how much it can hurt. Now that I'm an old woman, I must give birth to a new heaven, earth, and nations by my words instead of my womb. I use Isa. 66:6-9 as my mark as "the beast who was, and who was not, yet is" now in the flesh of a woman. I hope my truth will set you free, and you have at least a mustard seed of belief.

> Rev. 12:14 "And to the woman were given two wings of a great eagle, that she might fly into the wilderness, into her place, where she is nourished for a time, and times, and half a time, from the face of the serpent."

> Isa. 66:6-9 "A voice of noise from the city, a voice from the temple, a voice of the Lord that rendereth recompense to his enemies. Before she travailed, she brought forth; before her pain came, she was delivered of a man child. Who hath heard such a thing? Who hath seen such things? Shall the earth be made to bring forth in one day? Or shall a nation be born at once? For as soon as Zion travailed, she brought forth her children. Shall I bring to the birth and not cause to bring forth? saith the Lord: shall I cause to bring forth and shut the womb? saith thy God."

Finally, it is my honor to invite you all to a wedding designed to end all time. As well as inform you that just like the wedding in Cana when

Jesus Christ did his first miracle by changing the water to wine, He saved the best for these last days and times. Jesus always knew the Father would give him a wife. So just remember the parable below, and for your sakes, wear the right clothes!

Math. 22:2-13 "The kingdom of heaven is like unto a certain king, which made a marriage for his son, And sent forth his servants to call them that were bidden to the wedding: and they would not come. Again, he sent forth other servants, saying, tell them which are bidden, Behold, I have prepared my dinner. My oxen and my fatlings are killed, and all things are ready: come unto the marriage. But they made light of it, and went their ways, one to his farm, another to his merchandise: And the remnant took his servants, and entreated them spitefully, and slew them. But when the king heard thereof, he was wroth: and he sent forth his armies, and destroyed those murderers, and burned up their city. Then saith he to his servants, the wedding is ready, but they which were bidden were not worthy. Go ye therefore into the highways, and as many as ye shall find, bid to the marriage. So those servants went out into the highways, and gathered together all as many as they found, both bad and good: and the wedding was furnished with guests. And when the king came in to see the guests, he saw there a man which had not on a wedding garment. And he saith unto him, Friend, how camest thou in hither not having a wedding garment? And he was speechless. Then said the king said to the servants, bind him hand and foot, and take him away, and cast him into outer darkness; there shall be weeping and gnashing of teeth."

Rev. 19:9 "And he saith unto me, Write, Blessed are they which are called unto the marriage supper of the Lamb. And he saith unto me, these are the true sayings of God."

MY GENESIS

But please let me digress, as I need to take you back to when I found out who I am and how it all began. Our department mandated all employees attend positive attitude classes developed by the late Zig Ziglar, called See You At The Top (SYATT). Zig was a Christian minister and a republican motivational speaker. When I began the six-week one-hour classes taught by the deputy director, I was newly pregnant with my son. Attendees of the 25-person classes included all white managers and a staff of various backgrounds and religions. The classes referenced a lot of bible scripture. Although I am a Christian who agreed with Zig's principles, I felt like the classes itself was being taught from a white male, racist, and sexist viewpoint. I told them so too. Maybe it was my hormones or the fact that I have never really been known for holding my tongue. Especially after seeing some of the managers laughing at employees who, through tears at times, revealed their hidden sorrows or fears. Prior to graduation, we had to name our hero or shero and say why. I chose Maya Angelou and recited her "Still I Rise" poem. After graduation, I was committed to reading the whole bible for myself. I tried many times before, and by the next year, I finished it.

One day, I agreed with a Christian co-worker and aspiring minister to my 1st total 24-hour fast. She was convinced our troubles were due to Satan's bondage of women in our lives and the workplace. We began the fast at 12:00 pm on Thursday, and I never mentioned it to my husband. As I made dinner for him and our two kids, he did not even notice I was not smoking any cigarettes. After they went to bed, instead of eating, I read my bible and had finished Job 2 when my mind began to wonder. I asked myself a question, "What does the number 731 mean?" That number was always around me. It was either my phone number, license plate, or zip code, and it was the exact time my son was born less than a year earlier. I knew not to play it like a lotto number. Whenever I saw it while driving, it affirmed the thought I had in my mind at the time, or I was headed in the right direction. Well, after asking what 731 means,

I heard a little voice say to me, "Go back to the beginning." So, I did Genesis 1:1 until I reached all those begots and said to myself, "but I still don't understand." Then the same little voice said to me, "Begin again." So back to Genesis 1 I went. Time seemed to slow down, and I felt the urge to draw a big circle on the pad of paper to show the void and/or a zero, where all numbers come from. I split the circle, making the left side dark and leaving the right light. Like the face of a clock, I divided time by 12 hours to show two forms of water, aka H2O, as two holy omegas. I understood the numbers 1-26 and letters A-Z, when I heard a kind of mental "knock knock." I stopped reading and said to myself "God is that you, the Tree of Knowledge of Good and Evil? Is Jesus the tree of life and other tree of multiple fruits your wife?" Then I shut the Bible and reopened it to the first place I saw. This was a little trick my grandmother taught me to do. I opened it up to …

> Math 19:16-17 "Good Master, what good thing shall I do, that I may have eternal life? And he said unto him why calleth thou me good? There is none good but one, that is, God."

Well, that answered my question, but then I felt an evil presence around me. I shut my bible, threw it across the room, and commanded that presence to Get Out of My House!

> Math. 17:15-21 "Lord have mercy on my son for he is a lunatic … Howbeit this kind goeth not out but by prayer and fasting."

I guess that's why people say, "curiosity killed the cat", but satisfaction brought me back. While reading about the Garden of Eden, I felt like I was there too when the Serpent asked Eve what God said about eating of the trees. For some reason, this time Eve's reply really troubled me. She said in Gen. 3:3 they could "not eat <u>neither touch the tree</u> or they would die." Even a serpent, being the most subtle of all the beasts, knew the "neither touch" part was a lie. The only one Eve could have gotten this big fat fish story from was Adam, and her own husband. I reread

Gen. 2:17-3:3 part of the bible three times. Nowhere did God say anything about touching the tree. What came out of God's mouth, pure as can be, "Do Not Eat," was corrupted by the time it got to Eve. She obviously thought if she touched the tree, she would die. I decided to ask the book again, did I just see what I thought I saw? Was it really Adam's fault? I opened it up to the first place I saw.

> Luke 10:23-25. "Blessed are the eyes that see the things ye see; For I tell you many prophets and kings have desired to see those things which ye see; and have not seen them; and to hear those things which ye hear and have not heard them."

Whoa, I was on a roll and getting so good to me that I did it thrice but reopened it to the same gospel and prior scripture.

> Luke 10:21 "In that hour Jesus rejoiced in spirit, and said, I thank thee, O Father, Lord of heaven and earth, that thou hast hid these things from the wise and prudent, and hast revealed them unto babes. Even so, Father; for so it seemed good in thy sight. All things are delivered to me of my Father: and no man knoweth who the Son is, but the Father; and who the Father is, but the Son, and he to whom the Son will reveal him."

Now, I am grinning like a Cheshire cat because I'm not a man, and clearly just heard Jesus call me a babe. I was shocked to learn that out of 3 scriptures and 2 different gospels; all involved the same conversation.

But did you ever ask yourself, would a good God leave a newborn daughter in a garden with something that could harm them? No, a good God would leave someone wise like a serpent to watch them. So, lo and behold, if the whole truth be told, the serpent brought "light" to this fact. This was how Eve was beguiled, bewildered, or bewitched. How many times have you seen the Garden of Eden depicted with a big ass serpent wrapped around the tree? Most people notice Adam and Eve's belly buttons instead of the serpent touching the tree. Poor, poor Eve was just a babe in the woods, so to speak and had never seen a serpent before. Eve did not know serpents naturally touch trees, don't like fruit, and prefer flesh, blood, and meat. God told Adam about the Die If Eaten Tree (DIET). He could have at least made Eve's first Break-Fast in bed, but no, he made her get it for them both. Eve was hungry to know what God said or not. Before she sinned, she looked hard at the fruit but could only see its outside, which looked good. Eve could not see the evil inside the fruit or herself. She did not know that she, Adam, and we all are born perfectly "good and evil" just like the tree, and with the choice to obey or not. Luckily, before Eve broke her break fast she technically prayed about what God said and what she was told.

I laughed out-loud when God asked Eve, "What is this thou hath done?" I knew God knows all. God cursed the serpent, gave Adam rule over Eve and her pain in childbirth. What you didn't understand is that the serpent and Eve were both females and the daughters of God. Eve could see the serpent moving but could hear it talking through women's intuition. Enmity is always between a man's wife and his harlot, mother, or sister. Like the strife between Moses' wife and his sister or the sister wives of Isaac, Rebecca, and Leah. But that wimp of a man Adam, blamed God for giving him Eve in the 1st place. Since the beginning of time, Eve has been blamed for getting man kicked out of the Garden of Eden. The bible clearly says Adam knowingly sinned, but Eve was deceived. I realized that (ADAM), have lied to us. Most preachers and teachers of the bible will not admit when they do wrongs. Some men would rather fall on their own sword than admit they were defeated by a woman or don't know it all.

Rom. 3:4 "Let God be true and all men a liar."

Num. 23:19 "God is not a man that he should lie."

2 Thes. 2:11 "And for this cause God shall send them strong delusion, that they should believe a lie: That they all might be

damned who believed not the truth but had pleasure in unrighteousness."

I could hardly wait to share the results of my 1st 24 fast with my coworker. It was around 11:30, and the managers had left the office for an early lunch. I called my coworker to discuss the results. I was surprised by her reaction as she defended Adam. She blamed the serpent, whom most Christians know was Satan. She seemed pissed, and we argued before she admitted Adam was with her and the only one who could have told Eve what God said. I hung up the phone, and then it was as though I heard a voice say AttenHut! I stood up immediately from my desk and looked up like a soldier standing at attention. Then a "female and kind of angry voice" began to answer every question I had asked God in my life. I also saw a transmission of alphabetical principles and theories shown to me in what seemed like the twinkling of an eye. The voice kept saying over and over "and that's why and that's why" until it just stopped. I sat down at my desk, filled out a sick leave request, and put it on my boss's desk before I left.

I lived less than 20 miles away from home, and the ride was more or less a straight shot. It still was not 12:00 yet, so I couldn't drink, eat, or smoke. I was driving 60 mph on a 40 mph road. About five miles from home, Lisa Stansfield's song "I'm All Woman" came on the radio, and I began to cry. Now I am questioning why I'm crying. I am really not a crier type of woman. Then a big ass bumblebee flew in the driver's side window. I thought it went behind the collar of my blouse or down my back. I braked, pressing my back against the seat, trying to crush it. I made it home fine but never did find the bee. I think God sent it to slow me down from driving so fast. When I walked through the door, my husband was still home. He looked at me as if he could tell something was wrong before he asked if I was all right. I replied yes, not wanting to discuss it, so he left for work. We alternated days we picked up our kids from day care. It was his day to get them and fix dinner. I just sat on the living room couch staring out of my balcony window for hours, trying to understand the past events.

I finally mustered up enough strength to ask one more question. I sat at the dining room table with my Bible, pen, and paper at my side. Starting to cry, I asked God in my heart Who am I, and why did you show me all these things? I never opened the book, but the reply from the small voice was "Woman, Eve, the Bride of Christ and the Anti-Christ." I said WHAT! No God, not me, as immediate fear raced through my heart. Yet before the first tear fell or I gulped, I heard the small voice whisper in my ear the 23rd Psalm. "Yea though I walk through the valley of the shadow of death, I will fear no evil for I am with thee." The fear left, but felt like a bee sting, and I still cried a lot. The only time I recall ever crying that hard was at my dad's gravesite as the members of his fife and bugle corps played Taps. Ok, Ok, ok, I know I'm a woman. Like Eve, I am the mother of children, but I wasn't really sure about the bride of Christ part. I thought it was the church. It was that Anti-Christ part that really scared the shittim out of me. FYI, Shittim was the land where Moab lived, and type of wood used to make the Ark of the Covenant.

Exo. 25:10 and they shall make an ark of Shittim wood.

Num. 25:1 And Israel abode in Shittim and people began to commit whoredom."

I tried to deny what I heard. Surely, I Miss Understood, until I noticed I'd written it down on the pad. How could I explain it? WTF, I didn't understand, but somehow my spirit did. Who is the Anti-Christ or antichrists according to the Bible? God made one Jesus Christ and one Not or the Anti Christ, but since none of us is Jesus Christ, we all are antichrists. None of us comes out of the womb knowing who Jesus Christ is or was. We all are taught first, right?

1 John 2:18 "Little children it is the last time and ye have heard that Antichrist shall come. Even now are there many antichrists whereby we know that it is the last time.

1 John 2:22 "Who is a liar but he that denieth that Jesus is the Christ. He is the Antichrist that denieth the father and the son.

Once we know and accept the free gift of salvation Jesus offered at Calvary, we become Christians, a new creation, and are no longer antichrists. I was relieved to know that I had been baptized twice. Once, at Shiloh Baptist Church, when I was about 10 years old, and another time after I married my first husband. We eloped on April Fool's Day, but like Jesus he died unexpectedly at Holy Cross Hospital. Actually, I was happier than I had ever been. What woman wouldn't want to be the wife of Jesus Christ? Don't nuns consider themselves the brides of Christ? What Woman, Eve or Bride-to-be, would not tell Oprah, her friends, and use the World Wide Web like a Black Widow Spyder. I felt a hovering of pure love, peace, and protection around me for a week.

First, I decided to call my mother-in-law, who lived in New Bern, NC, and told her son had to leave my home because I was returning to Jesus Christ. We had been having problems for years, separated twice before, and my son was less than a year old. Then I called my mom in New Rochelle, NY, to tell her what I thought was really Good News and the miraculous things God showed me in the bible. How answers to the bible's mysteries were write before our eyes the whole time, and end with a win-win. About 5 hours later, my mom and sisters were at my house trying to convince my husband to get me some help. He didn't seem to think there was anything wrong and that I should stop just smoking pot. My mom thought I just needed to sleep for about a week. She said I was spitting out information like a computer. I didn't mention to him the things I had read or saw the Bible. I do recall he would say to me in jest, "Burnt you ain't nothing but the devil." Turns out he was right. As a result, I was put on some heavy medications that stopped me from dreaming, and I walked around like a zombie for weeks.

I never spoke to that coworker again. However, as A PAIN ND ASCC that I am did eventually sue my employer for RAPE RAGE (Religion, Ancestry, Political, Ethnicity, Race, Age, Gender, Equal Education and Employment) forms of discrimination. As it turned out, my tribe was the original landowner of my employer. Although I had "legal standing," the case was dismissed, as no attorney would represent me. I appealed to the US Supreme Court for an Extraordinary Writ of Man-Damn-Us but my pro se petition was denied, and I let the case expire. My employer never promoted me, but I did receive outstanding evaluations, bonuses, and paid leave off until I decided to retire. That was a result of the first Trump presidency. In any case, 40 years later and after studying the Bible, I can explain to you what has been kept hidden. As well as, how I became Satan now risen and reborn as the daughter of God, twin sister, and wife of Jesus Christ.

THE ALPHA BETA CHART DIE-A-LOGUE

The Alpha Beta Chart darkly and delightfully describes a dialogue between the 1ˢᵗ Alpha male, aka Jesus Christ, and the 2ⁿᵈ Beta female aka Satan that none knew existed. The ABC is a tool for you to use that shows you how words can change and the powers that they hold. The bible was translated from Hebrew, Greek, and Sanskrit languages into English. But the ABC uses English as the "End and Original" language spoken prior to God changing the language into babble. The ABC is like the board game Scrabble. It assigns each letter A-Z and numbers 1-26 a gender, power, position and place. The reader must know English principles and the difference between synonymous and syntax use to understand this long-hand form of writing. You must use your brain to be able to discern the metonyms and this form of Pig Latin. Here is an example of the words: KNOWLEDGE turns into (Know, Now, the No, L/ine, L/edge or Edge). The words "I AM" are all Ys or male, and the words "NOT GHOST" are all Xs or female. This ABC reveals the B/Read of Life and Hidden Manna promised by Jesus Christ.

> Rev. 2:17 "To him That overcomes will I give to eat of the hidden manna…"

New age thinking contends that the King James Bible is akin to his book on demonology. That the bible is a book of spells, which is why the first thing we teach our children is how to spell, read, and write. That the word gospel means God's spell so, the acts in the bible are scripts, then turned into scripture and/or a form of cryptology. As a result, many people want nothing to do with God, the bible or any form of indoctrinated religion. This book is for anyone who wants to know the whole truth before it is all said and done. I highly suggest you slow down your reading of the Bible as not to miss the signs you did before.

THE ALPHA-BETA CHART

A-M as in (I AM) Jesus Christ and N-Z as in (NOT) Jesus Christ

X(yX)X

1	2	3	4	5	6	7	8	9	10	11	12	13
A	B	C	D	E	F	G	H	I	J	K	L	M
Y	X	X	X	Y	X	X	X	Y	X	X	X	Y

14	15	16	17	18	19	20	21	22	23	24	25	26
N	O	P	Q	R	S	T	U	V	W	X	Y	Z
X	X	X	Y	X	X	X	Y	X	X	X	Y	X

A. Alpha Male, Abba, Ace, Adam and All males are 1st and Ys

B. Beta Female, Be, Bea, Bear, Beast, Bee, Beelzebub, and Beg, also the letters; b, d, and p are all female Xs. All females are the 2nd

C. Gamma, Trinity, 3 kinds of C's, Sea or See, as well as 3 kinds of Christ. One Jesus, One Anti-Christ, and rest antichrists or 3rd.

D. Delta, Dare, Dear, Deer, Deceiver, Devil, Disciples, 4 seasons, 4 Directions, and the smaller case letters b, d, and p and 4th

E. Epsilon, E speaks for itself or Example such as: B, C, D, G, P, T, V and Z. 5 fingers on hands, 5 toes on a Foot and 5th letter.

F. Digamma, Man made on the 6th Day, Fair, Fare and Fear. 6th

G. Zeta, Sabbath Day, words Holy Ghost are all Xs or female and show a complete week or 52 weeks a Year and 7th letter

H. Eta, Her, Hera, Hecate, Hand, Host/Hostess and H20 but if switched up-side down look the same as H, I, X and 8th letter

I. T/Heta, I, Eyes, a 6 or 9 if upside down made greater as a 9th

J. Tota, the difference between God's= X(yX)X left hand side and right positive one at Her right side of the zero,

18

K. King, with 2 Kinds of Kins Knowledge, silent Queen, 11th letter.

L. L/ine, between a man or woman, Lion/Lioness, Lady/Lord 12th

M.Ma, Maker, Male, Man, Mankind, Men, M-Other, and 13th letter.

THE ALPHA-BETA CHART

A-M as in (I AM) Jesus Christ and N-Z as in (NOT) Jesus Christ

X(yX)X

1	2	3	4	5	6	7	8	9	10	11	12	13
A	B	C	D	E	F	G	H	I	J	K	L	M
Y	X	X	X	Y	X	X	X	Y	X	X	X	Y

14	15	16	17	18	19	20	21	22	23	24	25	26
N	O	P	Q	R	S	T	U	V	W	X	Y	Z
X	X	X	Y	X	X	X	Y	X	X	X	Y	X

N. Nay, Negative (-1), No, Nosey, Not, Nothing, Nut and the difference between I Am Christ and I am Not Christ. 14th.

O. O(me)ga, Odd, Of, Off, Old, Omnipotent, On, One, Or, Orb, Other, Ox and difference between God and Good. 1/3 of 15th

P. People, Persons, Persona, Police, Politic, Pole, Poll, a President or P resident, as well as the smaller case p, d and b. 16th letter

Q. Queen, Queer, Quest and Question represent Y and 17th letter.

R. Read, Red, Read, Rear, Rare, as Repeat of letter 18th letter

S. Spirit, S/He is always present, able to S/witch to the left or right of word/s tuning them into a double-edged s/word. 19th

T. T/He symbol for the Cross Trinity, T/heir, T/here, Time 20th

U. Universe, "U" is You if Ys, Unity, 2 against 1 or 21st letter.

V. Vice, Victim, Victor, Valor, Veal, Viking and half a W, 22nd

W. We, Woman, Wild, Wise, Water, the W is double (Y)ou Men who look the same except upside-down M, 6 or 9, 2/3rds or 23

X. Unknown X, female gene in both men and women and the greater Trinity family=X(yX)X member. 24 hours a day 24th.

Y. Yahusha, Jesus or male in the trinity X(yX)X. He is the Y or reason Why God sent him 1st as son of God in the flesh. 25th

Z. A sideways N, End of Alpha-Bet Zach, Zeus, and Zion and 26th.

DIVINE TRINITY MOTHER FAMILY

Satan uses bible scripture "male and female made he them" along with Charles Mendel's Human Gender theory (Xy=males and XX= females) to prove we all come from the dark heavenly body, water and womb of a Goddess=X(y+X)X, or Mother instead of a Father. Due to the prominence of twin sons born in the bible, this X(y+X)X theory instead shows a Goddess with twin boy and girl within Her womb as the real Trinity. This X(y+X)X theory shows Jesus Christ as the only (y) or son of God and male and the center X a female as God's daughter Satan.

Jesus used many metonyms and parables in the bible. For example, the Trinity aka the Father, Son and Holy Ghost are One. Then the Mother, Daughter and Holy Ghostess is the other One that "bear witness in earth." When Jesus said "the father and I are one" he meant the X and y are one human and the mother and daughter XX are another. Not that he and the father were the same person. Individually the Father=X, Son=(y) and Mother=X and Daughter=X would be a qua-trinity not trinity. But as you can see all the Xs are female including the father. So, my X(y+X)X theory of the real Trinity is a biblical, literal, mathematical and scientific parallel analogy.

> Math. 28:19 "Go ye therefore and teach all nations baptizing them in the name of the Father and of the Son and of the Holy Ghost."

> 1 John 5:7 "For there are three that bear record in heaven the father the word and the holy ghost of and these three are one. And there are three that bear witness in earth the spirit, the water, and the blood and these three are one."

> Rev. 10:7 "But in the days of the voice of the 7th Angel when he shall begin to sound the mystery of God should be finished as he hath declared to his servants and the prophets."

So, as above so below the God parent of Jesus Christ is a female and the greatest family member. Although with God all things are possible, the fact is you can't have a father or son without a female mother or daughter. This is why the Virgin Mary was so important, and you were told that Joseph was not his father. This is also the reason Adam named Eve the "mother of all living" knowing he was the father of none.

Job. 17:14 "I have said to corruption thou art my father, to the worm, thou art my mother and my sister."

Job. 38:28 "Hath the rain a father or who has begotten the drops of dew? Out of whose womb X(y+X)X came the ice and the hoary frost of heaven who has gendered it?"

Mark 9:48 "Where the worm dieth not and the fire is not quenched

If (Father And Mother I Love You) means FAMILY, then I need to bring to your attention the turmoil caused to children in families. Don't you hate it when one parent favors one child over the other but will never admit they do? The bible clearly shows this kind of favoritism throughout the book. There was the favor of Able over Cain, the favor to Jacob by God who hated his twin Esau. The prodigal son over the elder, a son forsaken upon a cross, while younger even got away with murder. My view of twins Jesus Christ and Satan within God's spiritual womb X(y+X)X can be seen in Gen. 25 when God talked to Rebecca. Although she had sons I contend due to "male and female made he them" the bible describes the twins in God's womb as a boy and a girl. This view of the Trinity X(69)X uses 6 as the number of man and 9 as the number of woman made later like him but switched upside down.

Gen. 25:22"And the children struggle together within her, and she said if it be so why am I thus and she went to inquire of the Lord. And the Lord said unto her two nations are in thy womb and two manner of people shall be separated from thy bowels.

And the one people shall be stronger than the other people. And the elder shall serve the younger. And when her day to be delivered were fulfilled behold there were twins in her womb."

Surely the virgin Mary favored Jesus as opposed to Joseph his stepdad not so much. I'd bet Joseph's other kids made fun of him, called him names and even thought Joseph wasn't the father because they were all dark skin and Jesus was the lightest of the bunch. Remember how the other Joseph's (Gen. 37) older brothers threw him down a well trying to kill him because he was their father's favorite. How God made that baby boy so powerful Joseph eventually saved them and his whole family.

This view of the tree of life X(yX)X is another metonym that refers to the mother and daughter as the Holy Ghostess. The Tree of Life is female and shows the center X as God's pms blood Satan that naturally fell to the ground. Only a woman bleeds every month. Only water and blood come from a woman's womb. This is why God deemed Satan and the woman's time of the month as unclean.

1 John 5:7 "For there are three that bear record in heaven the father the word and the holy ghost of and these three are one. And there are three that bear witness in earth the spirit, the water, and the blood and these three are one."

Rev.22:2 "In the midst of the street of it, and on either side of the river, was there the tree of life, which bare twelve manner of fruits, and yielded **her** fruit every month: and the leaves of the tree were for the healing of the nations."

Daniel saw a woman and on the other side of the river, but he didn't understand what he saw.

Dan. 12:5-9 "Then I Daniel looked, and, behold, there stood other two, the one on this side of the bank of the river, and the other on that side of the bank of the river. And one said to the man clothed in linen, which was upon the waters of the river, how long shall it be to the end of these wonders? And I heard the man clothed in linen, which was upon the waters of the river, when he held up his right hand and his left hand unto heaven, and sware by him that liveth for ever that it shall be for a time, times, and an half. And when he shall have accomplished to scatter the power of the holy people, all these things shall be finished. And I heard, but I understood not. Then said I, O my Lord, what shall be the end of these things? And he said, go thy way, Daniel: for the words are closed up and sealed till the time of the end."

The Virgin Mary was a Her-Ma-Phradite and Jesus was inside her womb X(y+X)X all along. Mother (Mark 4:28) "earth bringeth forth fruit of herself." This means you never had a father in heaven. It has always been Mama's baby and Daddy's maybe. So, Jesus was Her son who died on the cross, and <u>no man</u> could claim to be his father. I doubt most people really believed the mother of Jesus was a virgin or that Joseph was not Jesus' father. Jesus couldn't tell you that our Father in heaven was female, nor could he tell you his Mother on earth wasn't a harlot. Instead, he said, look at him, knowing how much he favored his mother. The prophets in the bible saw their past, present day and future. Jesus is the leaven (yeast that make us rise) in his description of the kingdom of heaven and in consideration of my X(y+X)X theory.

Math.13:33 "…spake he unto them the kingdom of heaven is like unto leaven which a woman took and hid in three measures of meal until the whole was leavened."

Jer. 31:22 "How long will thou go about oh thou backsliding daughter for the Lord has created a new thing in the earth, a woman X(yX)X shall compass a man."

John 16:12-14 "I have yet many things to say unto you, but you cannot bear them now. How, be it when he the spirit of truth is come, he will guide you into all truth. For he shall not speak of himself but whatsoever he shall hear that shall he speak, and he will show you things to come. He shall glorify me for he shall receive of mine and show it unto you.

There is no T/Ruth without King David's or my grandma Ruth. Had Ruth not followed her mother-in-law's God; Jesus would not be called the root or son of David. Ruth is the only woman mentioned in the genealogy of Christ. Because the only blood in Jesus came from his mother. My real grandma was named Ruth. She and my grandfather were Masonic. She was an Eastern Star. Besides that, all men know especially David, the real kingdom of heaven is when they <u>come</u> into the womb of a woman.

Math. 25:1-13 "Then shall the kingdom of heaven be likened unto ten virgins, which took their lamps, and went forth to meet the bridegroom. And five of them were wise, and five were foolish. They that were foolish took their lamps and took no oil with them. But the wise took oil in their vessels with their lamps. While the bridegroom tarried, they all slumbered and slept. And at midnight there was a cry made, Behold, the bridegroom cometh; go ye out to meet him. Then all those virgins arose and trimmed their lamps. And the foolish said unto the wise, Give us of your oil; for our lamps are gone out. But the wise answered, saying, not so; lest there be not enough for us and you. But go ye rather to them that sell and buy for yourselves. And while they went to buy, the bridegroom came; and they that were ready went in with him to the marriage. And the door was shut. Afterward came also the other virgins, saying, Lord, Lord, open to us. But he answered and said, Verily I say unto you, I know you not. Watch therefore, for ye know neither the day nor the hour wherein the son of man cometh.

Luke 15:8-10 "Either what woman having 10 pieces of silver if she loses one piece does not light a candle, sweep the house, and seek diligently till, she finds it? And when she has found it, she called her friends and her neighbors together saying rejoice with me for I have found the pieces which I had lost. Likewise, I say unto you there is joy in heaven in the presence of the angels of God over one sinner that repenteth."

Below are several metonyms Jesus used relating to the number 10 and completion. Ten refers to the 10 fingers or toes on our hands or feet. On one hand, there were 5 wise virgins and on the other hand, 5 foolish. But God began the bible showing the importance of having two hands. Therefore, as with God's left and right hands, one hand was good and the other hand evil.

Math. 20:23 "But to sit on my right hand and on my left is not mine to give, but it shall be given to them for whom it is prepared by my father."

Math.6:3 "But when thou doest alms let not thy left hand know what thy right hand doeth that thy alms may be in secret."

Dan. 2:41-42 "The Kingdom shall be divided but there shall be in it as of the strength of the iron for as much as thou sawest the iron mixed with miry clay. And as the toes of the feet were part of iron and part clay so the Kingdom shall be partly strong and partly broken."

The numbers 1, 2, and 12, and how they relate to time itself. Think of the face of a clock. It has 1 hand called the long hand and the other, or the 2nd, is called the shorthand. Then God divided the darkness from the light, giving 12 hours of Dark, aka Midnight, and 12 hours of Light, called Noon or Mid Day. Six hours of Dusk and Six hours of Dawn So, 1 Hand is for God's sun/son, and the 2nd hand is God's moon or lunatic daughter. The third hand is called the second hand are the creation of the Y and X aka the angels or our children created by the dark and light. Then the evening and morning become one whole day. Just as one plus another one equals two.

Gen.1:2 "and darkness was upon the face of the deep. And the spirit of God moved upon the face of the waters. And God said, let there be light and there was light and God saw the light that it was good and <u>God divided the light from the darkness and God called the light day and the darkness he called night; and the morning and the evening and the morning were the first day."</u>

There are 12 hours in a day we should work and there are 12 tribes of Israel. There were 12 apostles, 12 loaves of showbread in the Tabernacle, 12 spies sent to scout the land of Canaan, 12 judges, 12 silver platters, 12 silver bowls, 12 golden pans, and the dedication of the Tabernacle, and there are 12 in a dozen.

God, Jesus, and Satan always existed as spirits within God's heavenly water and womb. With God, there was no need to have a father, only a mother. We are all born except Jesus from a father and a mother. God made up the story of a father and mother, so that at the End you would understand where you came from, which is from Her.

Are you ashamed of God because She is both our mother and father, or One God parent? If you can believe that Jesus Christ was a real man, born of a virgin woman, that he died for your sins and now sits at the right hand of God, then you should have no problem with Satan being the daughter of that same God. One for Him and Two for me, which as the Beta is double the Alpha male.

MYSTERY THE MOTHER OF HARLOTS AND ABOMINATION OF THE EARTH

Spiritually speaking, Jesus Christ and I are twin sisters and brothers. But, humanly speaking, we are half-brother and sister, just like with Abraham's wife, Sarah. Jesus was born of a virgin woman, and I was born of the mother of harlots in New Roc-Helle, NY. Have you ever noticed in your Bible that the mother of harlots and abomination of the earth is all capitalized? God has been shouting at us for a long time to recognize the importance of mothers whom men named as harlots. I, as the daughter, am the woman drunken with the blood of saints and martyrs of Christ. I ride the beast inside of me, kinda like Khalisi from the Game of Thrones HBO series.

> Hosea 1:2 "And the Lord said to Hosea go take unto thee my wife of whoredom and children of whoredom for the land has committed great whoredom departing from the Lord."

> Rev. 17:5 "On her forehead was the name written MYSTERY, BABYLON THE GREAT THE MOTHER OF HARLOTS AND ABOMINATIONS OF THE EARTH And I saw the woman drunken with the blood of Saints."

> Rev.18:7 "How much she has glorified herself and lived deliciously so much torment and sorrow give her for she sayeth in her heart I sit a queen and shall be no widow and shall see no sorrow."

In Gen. 38, there is a story about Tamar, who was the daughter-in-law of Judah. She married two of his sons, whom God killed before bearing them a son. She was promised the third son when he became of age. However, Judah reneged on his promise and later became a widower. Although Judah knew Tamar for years, on a trip to buy sheep, he saw Tamar on the road but didn't recognize her. He assumed she was a harlot because her face was covered, and she had put off her widow's garments. As payment Judah offered Tamar a kid from the flock he was about to buy. As collateral he offered Tamar his signet ring, the corde and the staff in his hand. They laid together but then Tamar later left the area keeping Judah's things. Tamar conceived and when it was obvious she was with child, Judah demanded she be brought before him and then burned alive for harlotry.

When Judah asked Tamar who was the father of her child she showed him his signet ring, cord, and staff. Judah changed his stance quickly after finding out he was the father, daddy, or pappy. Then he declared, "She is more righteous than I because I gave her not to Shelah, my son," and he knew her no more. And it came to pass in the time of her travail that behold twins were in her womb." At the time of their birth, one child put out his hand first. The midwife tied a scarlet ribbon on his hand before he withdrew it, and the other twin was born first. In this breach lay the seed of David's royal house and the distant advent of Christ. All twins X(69)X struggle in the womb for room. So, it is not because one child is good and the other evil.

As with Rebecca, these twins, the elder, ended up serving the younger instead of getting their rightful blessings from the fathers. These two examples, though separated by generations, mirror one another in striking ways. Both center on women whose wombs bore not only children but entire futures. Both contain moments of startling reversal, a younger brother surpassing the elder. A hidden plan that upheld human expectations. Tamar's daring act secured the lineage through which kings and the Messiah would come. Rebecca's direct audience with God revealed a prophecy that shaped the destiny of Israel itself. In each case, the drama unfolds around the mystery of twin sons struggling for a thought of primacy. Both stories reveal how God's purpose advanced through women's resolve and the hidden work of the womb. Men may bargain, delay or misunderstand but the divine plan moves through the bodies and decisions of women. They are the future within themselves. Judah failed Tamar yet the messiah's line passed through her courage. Isaac loved Esau, yet God loved Jacob, who was chosen as covenant bearer.

God has an affinity with wives and with harlots because God is a female too. God saved Rahab the harlot for helping the soldiers escape. Jesus Christ saved a harlot caught in adultery and from being stoned, alone.

GREAT MYSTERY REVEALED

The key to understanding the Bible's mysteries and love story, I claim, involves 5 verses of scripture. All are found in the very 1st book of Genesis. More remarkably, other versions of the Bible have these same scriptures without any words changed.

> Gen. 1:27 "So God created man in his own image in the image of God created he him male and female created he them."

> Gen. 2:21-22 "And the Lord caused a deep sleep to fall upon Adam, and he slept and he took one of his ribs and closed up the flesh instead thereof. And the rib which the Lord God had taken from man made he a woman and brought her unto the man."

> Gen.2:23-24 "This is now bone of my bone and flesh of my flesh she shall be called woman because she was taken out of man. It is for this cause the man is to leave his father and mother to cleave unto his wife and the two shall become one flesh."

All the verses except for Gen. 2:21-23 or the creation story are repeated many times throughout the bible, as with the scripture below.

> Math. 19:4 "And said unto them have you not read that he which made them in the beginning made them male and female. And said for this cause shall a man leave his father and his mother and shall cleave unto his wife and they twain shall be one flesh"

Eph.5:32 says on the above scripture "This is a Great Mystery, but I speak concerning Christ." Well, so do I. The mystery is that even Jesus Christ will have his own wife. Duh…You just didn't know how or why. The first reason is that the only thing God ever made that was not good is a man alone. The second reason is that Jesus is aka the second Adam and bridegroom to come. God created Eve from the rib bone of Adam and Satan was the rib bone inside of Jesus, all along.

Jesus could send Satan to and fro but she only left him for a season. As Jesus slept on the cross, God used the precious water and blood that fell from his head, his side, and his feet to the ground below to make his own wife. Just as was done with the first Adam. Satan was the pain in Jesus' side waiting to be born and have a human body of her own. That's why Jesus said in Eph. 5:29

"Eph.5:29 "For no man ever yet hated his own flesh but nourished it and cherished it, even as the Lord the church."

Rom. 12:4 "For we have many members in one body, and all members have not the same office. So, we being many are one body in Christ and every one member one of another having then gifts differing according to the grace that is given to us."

1 Cor. 15:38 "But God giveth it a body as it has pleased him and to every seed his own body. All flesh is not the same flesh but there is one kind of flesh of men another flesh of beast another of fish and another of birds... There is one glory of the sun and another glory of the moon and another glory of the stars for one star different from another in glory. So also, in the resurrection of the dead it is sown in corruption it is raised in incorruption."

You were told the church was the bride instead of being a real woman who was a member of the church, a member of his body, and the rib bone of his bone with a different office. Why in the name of God would a King of Kings or Lord of Lords not have a Queen or Lady of his own? Even God was married to Israel and then divorced her. Yes, her because Israel and Judah were called sisters, not brothers. God also complained of being treated as a wife.

Jer. 3:7-8 &14 "And I said after she had done all these things turn, thou unto me but she returned not, and her treacherous sister Judah saw it. And I saw one for all the cause whereby backsliding Israel committed adultery I had put her away and given her a bill of divorce. Yet her treacherous sister Judah feared not but went and played the harlot.… Turn old backsliding children sayeth the Lord for I am married unto you and I will take you one of a city and two of a family and I will bring you to Zion."

Jesus and I are the two of a family X(y+X)X, and I am the woman in a city. God chose the foolish things of the world to confound the wise, but I am both a good and evil or foolish and wise woman who built her house in Proverbs 9.

Prov. 9 "Wisdom has builded her house. She has hewn out her seven pillars she has killed her beast she has mingled her wine. She has also furnished the table she has sent forth her maidens she crieth upon the highest places of the city. Whosoever is simply let him turn in hither. As for him that wanteth understanding she sayeth unto him come eat of my bread and drink of the wine I have mingled. Forsake the foolish and live and go in the way of understanding … Give instruction to a wise man and he will be yet wiser. Teach a just man and he will increase in learning. The fear of the Lord is the beginning of wisdom, and the knowledge of the holy is understanding. For by **me** thy ways shall be multiplied, and the years of thy life shall be increased.… Stolen waters are sweet and b/read eaten in secret is pleasant but <u>he knoweth not that the dead are there and that **her** guests are in the depths of hell.</u>"

You also missed the whole point of the Noah's ark scriptures. Noah had to take all the animals **two by two**. The male and female of man, sheep, or beast. Noah and his wife and his sons and their wives. God first destroyed the world by water and promised this time by fire.

Luke 12:49-51 "I am come-to send fire on the earth and what will I-be if it already be kindled… suppose ye that I am come to give peace on the earth I tell ye nay but rather division."

I am hoping this book will spread like wildfire all over the world. Mostly because before Jesus went to the cross, I gave him my heart for safekeeping. So, I survived the stake of the cross, or it didn't hurt one bit. Technically, I took a dive, I took a fall, I was just playing dead, y'all. Like Sleeping Beauty, I was cast into a bed and told to play dead. After his death, Jesus went into hell to set the captives free. He raised me from the dead as he did for the ruler of the synagogue's daughter. I remind you, Jesus put out his disciples for not believing the daughter was asleep but dead and for laughing him to scorn. So in this part, I play the maid.

> Luke 8:52 "And all wept and bewailed her but he said weep not, she is not dead but sleeping. And they laughed him to scorn knowing that she was dead and he put them all out. And took her by the hand and called saying maid arise and her spirit came again. And she arose straight away, and he commanded to give her meat. And her parents were astonished but he charged them they should tell no man what was done."

> Rev.3:9 Behold I will make them the synagogues of Satan which say they are Jews and are not but do lie. I will make them to come to worship before thy feet and to know that I have loved thee."

So, Friends, Romans, Hebrews, or countrymen, lend me your ears to hear what the Spirit of Truth has to share. Jesus was the sin offering, but I am the burnt offering who comes in the volume of the book. According to below I also was sanctified by the blood shed by Jesus Christ. So, please repent and stop claiming the devil made you do it because God already knows you thought up all those sins on your own.

> Heb. 10:7-10 "Then said I lo (I come in the volume of the book it is written of **me**) to do thy will oh God. Above when he said sacrifice and offering and burnt offerings and offering for sin, thou wouldest not neither had its pleasure therein which are offered by the law. Then said he lo I come to do thy will oh God.

He taketh away the first that he may establish the second by the which will we are sanctified through the offering of the body of Jesus Christ once for all."

Christians know Satan was a defeated foe, but still say Satan is the God of this world. A lot of people wondered why God never got rid of Satan. The obvious answer is that God could send me back as the Spirit of Truth. Now praising God and Jesus Christ, who even saved my life. The Bible says we should be "wise as a serpent but harmless as a dove. So, when reading the bible, pay close attention to these words: Man, Woman, And, Or, Nor and Like. As such the only thing like a prince is a princess, the only thing like a lion is a lioness and only thing like a Holy Ghost is a Holy Ghostess. Also keep in mind when the bible says "no man" it does not mean nobody can or that a woman cannot.

Revelation 5 shows Jesus Christ, as a man, did not open the book or loose the seals. The one who opens the book is a woman, or his treacherous backsliding sister, aka the Lioness of Judah.

> Rev. 5:2-5 " And I saw a strong Angel proclaiming with a loud voice who is worthy to open the book and to loose the seals thereof and no man in heaven nor in earth neither under the earth was able to open the book neither to look there on and I wept much because no man was found worthy to open the book neither to look thereon and one of the elders sayeth unto me weep not behold the lion of the tribe of Judah the root of David has prevailed to open the book and to lose the seals"

Now this "little book" must be shared and taught all over the world. As the good book aka the Bible once so sweet in the mouth of preachers before, will now make their bellies sore.

> Rev. 10:9-11 "And I went unto the Angel and said unto him give me the little book. And he said unto me take it and eat it up and it shall make thy belly bitter, but it shall be in thy mouth sweet

as honey. And I took the little book out of the angel's hand and ate it up. And it was in my mouth sweet as honey. And as soon as I had eaten it thy belly was bitter, and he say unto me thou must prophecy again before many people, nations, and tongues...."

Luke 15:3-7 "And he spake this parable unto them saying what man of you having 100 sheep if he loses one of them does not leave the 99 in the wilderness and go after that which is lost until he finds it. And when he finds it, he layeth it on his shoulders rejoicing. And when he cometh home he calleth together his friends and neighbors saying unto them rejoice with me, for I have found my sheep that was lost. I say unto you that likewise joy shall be in heaven over one Sinner that repenteth more than over the ninety-nine just person which need no repentance."

Jesus like Bo Peep, lost 1 in 100 black sheep in the Trinity family. He went looking for her and found me. He picked me up, washed me clean, put me on top of his shoulders, and we married. He took me home but then left me alone wagging this tale behind me. Isn't it funny how first men cleave unto their wife and then leave the rest unto their wives.

YOUR MAMA IS SO FAT

I've heard it said, "It ain't over until the fat lady sings." Well, the Fat Lady aka God Almighty, already sent Her son, and they killed him. This time God cast down with great anger her boney daughter, Satan, like a trump card she had up her sleeve all along. In the beginning, God showed Her face as darkness as Her spirit moved upon the waters. Then God said, "Let there be light," or whites. But did you know that God aka our Momma, is as fat and black as Aunt Jemima, grinning at us on the pancake box years ago. In fact, our momma is so fat even Jesus Christ himself calls her our fat-her who art in heaven. I'm more like Job's boney daughter Kizzie from the "Roots" TV series, which means in African "Stay Put." So as the Woe of man, Witch or (Daughter of God) men treat like Dogs, I am the black Bitch who set you sons of guns up for this Fall.

> Jer. 8:19-21 "Behold the voice of the cry of the daughter of my people because of them that dwell in a far country. Is not the Lord and Zion? Is not her king in her? Why have they provoked me to anger with their graven images and with strange vanities? The harvest is past, the summer is ended, and <u>we</u> are not saved. For the hurt of the daughter of my people, am I hurt? I am black, astonishment has taken hold of me."

> Job. 42:14 "And he called the name of the first Jemima and the name of the second Kizzia and the name of the third Kerenephia.

That is short for Karen's. I would be remiss not to mention Hagar, the mother of Abraham's firstborn son. She was the handmaiden of his wife, Sarah. We never received an inheritance like Job's daughters, due to our gender and former slave status. That's why the bible says "the first shall be last and the last shall be first" to inherit the kingdom.

> Gal. 4:22-25 says "For it is written that Abraham had two sons. The one by a bond maid and other by a free woman. But he who

was born of the bond woman was born after the flesh. But he of the free woman was by a promise which things are an allegory. For there are two covenants the one from Mount Sinai <u>which gender to bondage</u> which is Hagar. <u>For Hagar is Mount Sinai in Arabia to Jerusalem which now is in bondage with her children.</u>"

1 Corinthians 13: 9-12 "For we know in part and we prophecy in part, but when that which is perfect is come, then that which is in part shall be done away with. When I was a child, I spoke as a child, I understood as a child, I thought as a child, but when I became a man, I put away childish things. For now, we see through a glass darkly, but then face to face. Now I know in part, but then shall I know even as also I am known. And now abide in faith, hope and charity. These three things but the greatest of these is charity"

Thomas Jefferson warned us that God's justice would not sleep forever. But I was born of another promise, aka the Pledge of Allegiance. I was promised "One nation, under God, indivisible with Liberty and Justice for All." Now we have a 34-count felon residing in the White House as our president, selling his Bible as better than ours. These sons of guns still act like they know not what they have done in the name of the Lord. White men stole religion from the black Moors all over the world. Then changed the names and whitewashed Jesus aka Yahusha into a blonde-haired, blue-eyed man with a good tan. Well, I know what they meant for evil God meant for good. So, woe to you, mega church leaders, preaching prosperity instead of the great and terrible day foretold. You have become holier-than-thou lukewarm Christians. They would rather cover up the breast of Lady Justice because it offends them, instead of removing the blindfold that severely handicaps and retards her abilities. When is it her turn to wield the double-edged sword, she alone holds, aka the word of God? Christians are offended by curse words like ass, damn, hell, or shit, but make up euphemisms for them like sugar, honey, iced tea.

Jer. 8:11" For they have healed the hurt of the daughter of my people slightly saying peace peace when there is no peace. Were they ashamed when they had committed abominations? <u>Nay they were not at all ashamed neither could they blush.</u> Therefore, shall they fall among them that fall at the time of their visitation. They shall be cast down sayeth the Lord."

Job 2:4 "And Satan answered the Lord and said skin for skin, yea all that a man has will he give for his life. But put forth thy hand and touch his flesh and his bone and he will curse thee to thy face. And the Lord said unto Satan behold he is in thy hand but save his life Then Satan went forth and stuck Job with boils…. Then said his wife doth thou still retain thy integrity, curse God and die."

So, my message is to Donald Trump, Elon Musk, and all of you, Simon Peter, pumpkin eaters who have wives but couldn't keep them, prepare to separate the wheat from the tares, as one greater than the queen of the south is here. I am the queen in heaven who likes cake, Lady Justice and the Lady of the Lake who holds a double-edged sword like Excalibur. Or just "eat, drink and be merry, for tomorrow we die."

Math. 12:42 "The queen of the South shall rise up in the judgment with this generation and condemn it. For she came from the uttermost parts of the earth to hear the wisdom of Solomon and behold a greater than Solomon is here.

Jer. 7:18 "The children gather wood and the father's kindled the fire and the woman knead their dough to make cakes to the queen in heaven…"

Luke 22:31 "Simon behold, Satan has desired to have you that he may sift you as wheat."

God had to play both roles. She was the tree of the knowledge of good and evil. The father, who is God of war, strict and distant, versus the loving mother and quiet comforter who feeds you from her own body. The commandment was to honor thy father and mother, not one over the other. Satan is the tree of life since she is a Her and Jesus was the tree of multiple fruits Adam ate before eating from the tree of knowledge of good and evil. Had Adam and Eve not eaten of the tree, there would be no evil in the world. So, there would be no need for a bible. God is the first one to use the word evil and said the below in

> Isa. 45:7 "That they may know from the rising of the sun, and from the West, that there is none beside me. I am the Lord, and there is none else. I form the light and create darkness. I make peace and create evil; I the Lord do all these things.

To maintain power, men have ignored the woman's role or part that God Almighty prepared for them. Thankfully, the Bible didn't.

> Math. 4:4-10 "But he answered and said it is written man shall not live by bread alone but by every word that proceedeth out of the mouth of God ... Get thee hence Satan for it is written thou shall worship the Lord thy God and him only shall thou serve."

> Math.16:23 "Be it far from the Lord this shall not be unto thee. But he turned and said unto Peter, get thee behind me Satan thou art an offense unto me for thou severest not the things that be of God but those that be of men."

> John 21:22 "Jesus sayeth unto him if I will that he tarry till I come what is it to thee?

Jesus told Satan to get behind him, so you really should have been expecting me next. I guess I'm not quite what you were expecting, huh? Besides that, isn't the best defense a good offense? So after the fall, we will get a new heaven, and earth and Hell will be changed into a lake.

GOD'S DIRTY WORK

How many times did God use the Serpent, Angel of the Lord, or Satan to carry out God's commands? I can count at least eight. But that's how I know now is the time for the sons of the Ninevites to rise. One might think that, as Satan, I can do all kinds of miracles. But I lost all my powers at Calvary Cross. This is why Jesus said the below.

> Math 12:39 "But he answered and said unto them this evil and adulterous generation seeketh after a sign and there shall no sign be given it but the sign of the prophet of Jonas. The men of the Nineveh shall rise in judgment with this generation and shall condemn it because they repented at the preaching of Jonas…"

The first time God used the Serpent, to convince Eve to eat of the tree of knowledge of good and evil, and as the Angel of the Lord used to guard the garden so that they could not partake of the tree of life. Secondly, when God turned Moses's staff into a serpent that ate up the pharaoh's serpents, third, when God told Moses to make a serpent of brass so that those who were bitten by the fiery serpents would live, the fourth was when Balaam rode his she ass, and the Angel of the Lord was standing in his way. Balaam struck the ass 3 times until God opened her mouth. "The Angel of the Lord said to Balaam, had she not turned away, then surely, I would have killed you," and saved her black she ass alive.

The fifth was to test Job on the day of the Lord, but did you notice that it actually was a tie? Yes, a tie because Jobs' wife was also considered his flesh and bone. Job's wife said exactly what Satan said she would say, "Curse God and die." So, although it wasn't Job who sinned, his wife turned this test into a tie. Sixth, when God sent the Angel of the Lord, aka the Angel of Death, to kill the 1st born of Egypt and the beast. The Seventh is when God sent Satan to the wilderness to test Jesus. She didn't appear to him as a serpent, but as an adorable, angelic, beautiful, dark, and mysterious woman. Especially since that's the only thing that a 30-

plus-year-old virgin male had not had yet. Satan obviously had all the power given to her by God. She said Just bow down and worship me.

Math. 4:9 "And he sayeth unto him all these things will I give thee if thou will fall down and worship me."

Luke 10:18 "And he said unto them I beheld Satan as lightning fall from heaven."

Eighth, Jesus said that he beheld Satan as falling light from heaven. But what happens first, the thunder or the lightning, or is it worse? I hope the voice talking to you right now strikes you as lightning, and I have hit my target. Ninth, as we are in these last days and times, the only sign that will be given is the sign of Jonas. Now is the time for the sons of women aka the 9 vites to rise and repent like the people of Nineveh.

Jonah 3:4 "And Jonah began to enter the city a day's journey, and he cried and said yet 40 days and Nineveh shall be overthrown. So, the people of Nineveh believe God and proclaimed the fast and put on sackcloth from the greatest of them even to the least..."

Rev. 2:24 "But unto you I say and unto the rest in Thyatira, as many as have not this doctrine and which have not known the depths of Satan as they speak, I will put on you none other burden."

Almighty "God is a God of Order." From the very beginning, ever since God said, Let there be Light Her sun/son came forth, but the moon, or God's lunatic daughter, also in the darkness understood it not. I do not know who in their right mind would claim to be Satan unless they are sure that's who they are. So, I guess I'll will have to play the hand that's been dealt like my life depended on it.

WOMEN SAVED OR RISEN FROM DEAD

Three different Marys witnessed the crucifixion of Jesus. Mary, the mother of Jesus, Mary Magdalene, and Mary of Bethany. Mary Mag was the 1st one to see Jesus risen from the dead. However, the other disciples didn't believe her. Every time Jesus uses the words: woman, daughter, maiden, or mother he is speaking directly to you, if you are a female. Even if he refers to you as a Dog instead of a Daughter of God. The miracles Jesus performed on women are very important scriptures not usually heard in church. Jesus cast 7 demons out of Mary (Luke 8:2), but she was not a harlot nor the wife of Christ. But maybe she was called a harlot because they were very close friends and not married.

> Mark 7:27-29 "But Jesus said unto her let the children first be filled. For it is not meat to take the children's bread and to cast it unto dogs. And she answered and said unto him yes Lord, yet the dogs under the table eat of the children's crumbs. And he said unto her for this saying go thy way the devil is gone out of the daughter.

> Luke 13:11-16 "And behold there was a woman which had a spirit of infirmity 18 years and could not in no wise lift herself up. And when Jesus saw her, he called her to him and said unto her <u>woman</u> thou art loosed from thou infirmities. And he laid his hands on her and immediately she was made whole and glorified God. And the rulers of the synagogue answered with indignation because Jesus healed on the Sabbath…The Lord answered him and said thou hypocrite does thou not each of you on the Sabbath lose his ox or his ass from the stall and lead him away to the watering. And ought not this <u>woman</u> being a <u>daughter of Abraham whom Satan</u> has bound low these 18 years be loosed from bond on the sabbath day.

I caught him asleep with his rod or staff in hand, comforting himself, and tried to tempt him from going to the cross. I even offered some head, but he said, "Woe to women who give suck." All he had to do was get down on one knee and ask for my hand in holy matrimony. Instead, he defeated me at Calvary, gave me my own body, washed me clean with his blood, and married me. **What a son of man!** This way, Jesus will have an angel in his arms in the morning and the devil in his arms at night.

The only time his virtue was lost was when the unclean woman with what the Bible called a "private issue of blood" touched the hem of his robe. Jesus made a big fuss about a friendly game of touch football between a brother and sister with the same father or mother.

> Luke 8:43 "And Jesus said who touched me? When all denied Peter and they that were with him said master the multitude thronged the and press thee and sayeth thou who touched me? And Jesus said somebody touched me for I perceive that virtue has gone out of me… And he said unto her daughter be of good comfort thy faith has made thee whole go in peace.

> John 4:7 "Jesus sayeth unto her give me to drink for his disciples were gone away unto the city to buy meat. Then sayeth the woman of Samaria unto him how is it thou being a Jew asketh drink of me a samarian for the Jews have no dealing with the Samaria. Jesus answered and said unto her, if thou knew the gift of God, and who it is thou sayeth to thee, give me drink thou would have asked of him and he would have given the living waters. And the woman sayeth unto him Sir thou has nothing to draw with and the well is deep from whence then hast thou that living water... Then the woman sayeth unto him Sir give me this water and I thirst not neither come neither to draw she is the said unto her go call thy husband and come hither and the woman answered and said I have no husband Jesus said unto her thou hast well said I have no husband. Well thou hast had five husbands…."

Acts 9:36 Tabitha Interpretation is called Dorcas. This woman was full of good works and arms deeds which she did. And it came to pass in those days, that she was sick and died who when they had washed, they laid her in the upper chamber... Then Peter arose and went with them when he was come, they brought him to the upper chamber and all of the widows stood by him weeping and showing the coats and garments which Dorcas had made while she was with them. But Peter put them all forth and then nailed down and prayed and turning him to the body said Tabitha arise then she opened her eyes and when she saw Peter she sat up."

VOICES OF OTHER ANGELS

Have you ever heard a song that made you rejoice or cry although you didn't know why? Or songs you felt were talking to you directly. For me, the lyrics are as important as the melody. The Beatles songs "Let It Be," "Bridge Over Troubled Waters," and "For Every Turn" on Eccl. 3 comes to mind. I love Phil Collins "In the Air Tonight". I considered women like Mya Angelou's "Been Found" CD and "Still I Rise" poem, Whitney Houston's "I'm Every Woman", Diana Ross' "Love Hang Over", and Chaka Khan's "Through the Fire" are all Angels who sang me songs, poems, and psalms. In my mind, I picture Jesus' mother singing to him on the cross until his death, the "I Will Always Love You" song from the "Bodyguard." Now that song still makes me cry.

So, before you judge me, ask yourself this question. What would you do if you were me and believed God told you all these things? What if you were the Virgin Mary, Moses, or Jonas, would you obey God or not? God wants none to be lost, but eventually the wolf must show up. So, as God's lunatic daughter of I am still in charge of moon times, seasons, and tides.

> Eccl. 3:1-23 "To everything there is a season and a time to every purpose under the heaven. A time to be born and a time to die, a time to plant and a time to pluck up that which is planted. A time to kill and a time to heal, a time to break down and a time to build up. A time to weep and a time to laugh. A time to mourn time to dance...17. I said in my heart God shall judge the righteous and the wicked. For there is a time for every purpose and for every work. I said in my heart concerning the state of the sons of men that God might manifest them and that they might see that they themselves are beast. For that which befalleth the sons of men befalleth beast. Even one thing befalleth them as one dieth so dieth the other yeah, they have all one breath so that a man has no preeminence above beast for all is vanity."

There was another old song that says, "The whole world is a stage, and everybody plays a part. So, the stage is set, the curtain goes up," the scene is a nation full of broken promises and hearts.

SATAN'S DAY IN COURT

Satan is just A PAIN ND ASCC, like the widow in Luke below. She wants to Sioux/Sue her employer and government by putting her two cents worth in under sworn testimony. She drives her car into the federal court parking lot, and the guard notes her license plate that says "IMAGOD2." Satan is nervous about going to Court without a lawyer because no one would agree to provide counsel on her case.

> Luke 18:3 "There was a certain judge, which feared not God, neither regarded man: And there was a widow in the city; and she came unto him saying, Avenge me of mine adversary."

> Luke 21:2-4 "And also a certain poor widow casting in thither two mites." (cents or mights). "And he said, of truth I say unto you, this poor widow hath cast in more than they all; for these have of their abundance cast into the offering of God, but she of her poverty hath cast in all the living that she had."

She imagines throwing the Bible back into the Court and almost hits the Judge. She contends the 1st Amen-dment's "no law respecting an establishment of religion" is a Shame Before Almighty God! Also, a breach of contract, promise, and oaths that were all sworn on the Bible and form of Mass Religion Fraud. She says the GOP sold their souls to a Don't Tread On Me" Serpent spirit of independence flagpole. Further, woe to hypocritical men who put a blindfold on Lady Justice. She wants her turn to wield the Double-Edged Sword; she holds which is aka the word of God. The bible says, "they hated Jesus without a cause" and black people just because. Satan contends women need their own Declaration of Independence. That God made man first and "all men are created equal," but women made second were created better than men. So, her prayer to the Court is for a Her-It-Age to begin. She requests 1/3 credit for every penny and legal tender that has "In God We Trust" on it. As his wife, she is entitled to 2/3rds credit for damages.

Luke 20:24 "Shew me a penny, Whose image and superscription hath it? They answered and said Caesar. And he said unto them, Render therefore unto to Caesar the things which be Caesar's and unto God the thing which be God's.

PRESENTED QUESTIONS

What is the name of God We Trust: Allah, the Almighty Buck, I Am, Jesus Christ or God Damn?

Answer   I Am, that I Am

Do you think God would approve of the First Amendment which was freely sworn upon the Holy Bible before the US All?

Answer   No, do you.

What kind of fruit was on the tree of knowledge of good and evil?

Answer   I say it was a Pear tree for the following reasons. It was because p/ears have ears-and they heard what God said Don't Eat. Also, good and evil have always been a pair, just opposite sides or heads and tails of the same coin. Finally, due to the first day of Christmas song that goes and a Part/ridge in a pear tree.

Why did God turn Lot's wife into a pillar of salt?

Answer   Women are the salt of this earth and when we look back, we become bitter at the treatment of God's daughters. So, if the salt has lost its seasoning, what the hell good is it?

Why did the woman pour expensive oil on the feet of Jesus?

Answer   So that kick to my head would make his foot slip and it would not hurt one bit.

Why did Jesus obey the demons that asked to go into the pigs or swine that the Bible called the "sea, water or drink"?

Answer   Pigs have 30-minute-long orgasms, which is why they squeal so much. They will be on the wedding menu as a spirited drink and pigs in a blanket.

Which came first, the chicken or the egg?

Answer   Neither. The rooster was first. He crossed the road, knocked the hen up, then went back home to watch Monday night football. Leaving her to raise that poor chick all alone. She took that jailbird to court, asking for child support. But her case was dismissed because even the judge confessed that he couldn't understand hen talking women.

Why did Job say "I have said to corruption thou art my father, I have said to the worm thou art my sister and my mother"?

Answer   To let you know that, like the worm that never dies, neither does the mother, sisters, or daughters as they all are females.

What did Adam and Eve look like?

Answer   Adam was tall and Dark as the evening night, but Eve was drop dead gorgeous as the morning light. That is why black men are attracted to fairer-skinned ladies and refer to them as red bones.

Why did Cain kill Abel?

Answer   Due to basic sibling rivalry, Abel told Cain a lie. Abel said God liked him better because he was younger and light like his mama. Cain was angry but didn't mean to kill him. I recall hitting my younger sister over the head with a 7UP bottle. She got a little bump.

What did Jesus look like?

Answer   Well, Joseph, Mary, and his brother and sisters were very dark, but Jesus, being the way, truth, and life, was also the lightest in the bunch. That's how his siblings all knew

Joseph wasn't his real father and they thought he was adopted.

Why did the Bible say it will come as a snare upon the whole world?

Answer   Because for the very first time they will have to seriously listen to the voice of a woman. All this time, they thought Satan was a boy instead of a girl.

Did Jesus ever lie?

Answer   "Let God be true in all men a liar." And "God is not a man that he should lie." So, yes, Jesus Christ as a man, told a lie when he told people to pray our fat-her who art in heaven.

AND LIVED HAPPILY, FOREVER AFTER

Due to God's master plan, most Mother Goose or fairytales end with, and they lived happily ever after. Female children are taught that someday their prince will come and choose an adorable girl like them. But, at no time are they told they had a choice to say yea or nay without the father's permission. As with Cinderella, Sleeping Beauty, and Snow Queen, I am the Ugly Duckling transformed into a Black Swan. I know Jesus, and I will live happily forever after the Fall. I praise Almighty God each and every day for preparing a special place for me.

But one thing for sure is when the Son of God, aka the Lamb, gets back in town and this boney lioness lies down, I can't promise I won't lick my lips, give him a kiss, and damn near eat his ass up. I recall when I was told who I was, I just said, What! But that was because of being the Anti-Christ part. One may think this book is just a sick joke, but I am dead serious about what I wrote.

Please note: I neither expect nor want anyone to bow down or worship me because that would be wrong. I am just your fellow servant of God's. However, like the retuned prodigal son, I was given the best robe, aka my wedding dress, y'all. So, I am also entitled to receive a new heaven, earth, kingdom, mansion, rock of a ring, from my king, plus a bunch of maids and servants. And that's more than enough for me.

> Rev. 19:7-10 "Let us be glad and rejoice and give honor to him for the marriage of the lamb has come and his wife has made herself ready. And to her it shall be granted that she be arrayed in fine linen clean and white for the fine linen is the righteousness of saints…. And I fell at his feet to worship him, and he said unto me see thou do it not. I am thy fellow servant and of thy brethren that have the testimony of Jesus: worship God for the testimony of Jesus is the spirit of prophecy.

Rev. 7:17 "For the lamb which is in the midst X(y+X)X of the throne shall feed them and shall lead them unto living waters fountains of waters and God shall wipe all the tears from their eyes."

Whether you want to believe this or not we are all gods because God said we are. But if any part of this book has made you laugh or cry, I hope you realize it was the God in you who wiped away the tears from your eyes.

THE WEDDING TO END ALL TIME

It is my pleasure and honor to formally invite you to the wedding designed to end all time. All are welcome to attend but you must follow strict protocols. Guests of the groom sit on the right, and guests of the bride sit on the side left. Be sure to wear the right clothes (white linen) as you don't want to be put out for not. Then, when you hear the trumpets sound, something like Dum Dum Dedum, you rise because Here Comes the Bride, all dressed in white.

Jesus saved the best for the last days and times and changed the water into new wine. So those swine he cast into the sea or water will be on the wedding menu as a spirited drink and as pigs in a blanket. At the 1st wedding in Cana the mother of Jesus, was drunk and bugging him about when he would get married and give her some grand babies.

John 2:3-9 "when they wanted wine the mother of Jesus said unto him, they have no wine. Jesus said unto her woman what have I to do with thee, my hour is not yet come….7. When the ruler of the feast had tasted the water that was made wine and knew not whence it was but the servants which drew the water knew, the governor of the feast called the bridegroom and sayeth unto him every man at the beginning does for set forth good wine and when men have well drunk then that which is worse but thou hast kept the good wine until now".

2 John 1:1 "The elder unto the elect lady and her children whom I love in the truth and not only but also all that have known the truth… And now I beseech the lady not as though I wrote a new commandment unto thee but that which we had from the beginning that we love one another."

Rev. 22:16-17 "I Jesus have sent my Angel to testify unto you these things in the churches I am the root and the offspring of David and the bright and morning star. And the spirit and the bride say come and let him that heareth say come …."

So don't forget to RSVP this invitation to a Wedding Designed To End All Time, because It Will Be To Die For!

THE END

www.ingramcontent.com/pod-product-compliance
Lightning Source LLC
Chambersburg PA
CBHW051556120626
46551CB00013B/1539